5 MINUTES A DAY MANIFESTATION JOURNAL FOR WOMEN

21 DAYS OF GUIDED AFFIRMATIONS, MEDITATIONS, AND WRITING PROMPTS,

Using the Law of Attraction to release limiting beliefs and unleash the life of your dreams.

by Emery Pace Archer

WELCOME

Welcome to the *5 Minutes a Day Manifestation Journal for Women: 21 Days of Guided Affirmations, Meditations, and Writing Prompts.* This journal is a guided practice using the Law of Attraction to release limiting beliefs and unleash the life of your dreams.

This book is a lighted path for those ready to embark on a transformative journey that will guide you through self-discovery, empowerment, and boundless manifestation.

It aims to empower women like you to tap into your inherent power, cultivate deep-seated self-love, and use the Law of Attraction to manifest the life, love, and abundance you've always desired. This book is your map to doing just that.

As Louise Hay said in *You Can Heal Your Life*, "Every thought we think is creating our future." Let's start creating the future of your dreams now.

Why this book; why now? In an age where the clamor of external voices can drown out our inner guidance, finding a true sense of self and purpose can seem insurmountable.

Yet, within this very challenge lies our most incredible opportunity: to harness our inherent power, cultivate deep-seated self-love, and use the Law of Attraction to manifest the life, love, and abundance we've always desired.

In *The Power of Intention*, Wayne Dyer said, "Change the way you look at things and the things you look at change." This book is your map to doing just that.

Within these pages lies a carefully curated collection of guided meditations, energy-shifting affirmations, and inspirations for written reflection, each designed to be engaged for just five minutes daily.

This approach is rooted in the understanding that transformation doesn't require monumental changes overnight but instead, small, consistent acts of self-love and intentionality. This book is designed to be the strategy that guides you, gently but powerfully, toward your highest self.

Embracing the wisdom of habit research, we understand that it takes at least 21 days to create any perceptible change in a mental image.

Here, then, is a 21-day challenge: to shift your mindset, break free from limiting beliefs, and step into a space where you can manifest the life of your dreams.

It is not just about dreaming.

It's about making those dreams a tangible reality through dedicated practice and belief in the power of your thoughts and energies.

As we journey together through the next 21 days, you will be introduced to the foundational principles of the Law of Attraction:

Ask

Know that when you ask,
it is given.

Feel how it feels when it
is already done.

Experience it emotionally
and in all five senses
before it arrives.

Express gratitude or
appreciation that it is
done.

Picture clear images or
narrate them to yourself.

Find matching vibrations
and feelings, no matter
how small, throughout
your day.

Remember that receiving
is the path of least
resistance.

Be eager, open, flexible,
and allowing.

Receive

Using these principles,
you'll learn how to
effectively ask the
universe for what you
desire, believe in the
inevitability of your
success, and be open to
receiving abundance in
various forms.

The activities and
exercises are designed to
be introspective, allowing
you to peel back the
layers of your
consciousness, confront
your fears, and ultimately
find a wellspring of joy
and fulfillment.

Over the next 21 days, your journey will be one of exploration, transformation, and manifestation.

Each affirmation, meditation, and writing prompt will take no more than five minutes. I hope you will experience the profound impact just a few moments of dedicated practice can have on your overall well-being and life trajectory.

You will find a holistic approach to personal development and manifestation, starting with an empowering affirmation to rewire your default energy. Next, a guided meditation will align the mind and spirit. Finally, a writing prompt takes it a step deeper to discover and process thought patterns and desires as you align the inner with the outer.

For the greatest impact, complete at least 5 minutes daily for a minimum of 21 days. You can always add minutes or days any time you choose!

As you delve into this journey, remember that the universe always conspires in your favor. This book is the first step towards a remarkable transformation—one that will see you release limiting beliefs and embrace a life filled with love, abundance, and fulfillment.

Embrace this journey with an open heart and mind, and watch as the world opens up to you in ways you never thought possible.

Remember, as you embark on this 21-day adventure, "Small changes often will compound into remarkable results," a reminder from James Clear that even the most minor step taken today can lead to profound changes in your life.

Let this be the moment you choose to take control of your destiny, using the tools and wisdom shared within these pages to manifest the life you've always dreamed of.

WELCOME TO YOUR NEW BEGINNING.

This book is organized into three sections. You can follow the order below and complete each section in order. You can also dive into any section or activity that appeals to you. Follow your desire!

EMBARK

Self-Discovery and Releasing Limiting Beliefs

EXPAND

Visualization and Affirmation for Empowerment

EXEMPLIFY

Action and Manifesting Your Dreams

EMBARK

SELF-DISCOVERY AND RELEASING LIMITING BELIEFS

IDENTIFYING LIMITING BELIEFS

1

I AM | I WILL | I CAN
I HAVE | I APPRECIATE

I AM OPEN TO
DISCOVERING MY TRUE
SELF BEYOND MY
BELIEFS.

AFFIRMATION

I AM | I WILL | I CAN
I HAVE | I APPRECIATE

MEDITATION

Sit comfortably and close your eyes. Begin by taking deep, conscious breaths. Inhale positivity; exhale negativity. Visualize a stream of light entering your body with each inhale, cleansing and opening your heart and mind. As you settle into this space of openness, ask yourself gently, "What beliefs limit my infinite potential?" Allow these beliefs to surface without judgment, observing them as clouds passing in the sky of your mind. With each exhale, imagine these limiting beliefs dissolving into the light, leaving you clear and open.

WRITING

Identify your most present limiting beliefs. What is holding you back deep down? Ask why, and why again. Go deeper. Reflect on these beliefs. Consider their origins. Are they from past experiences, societal expectations, or self-imposed narratives? Write about how these beliefs have shaped your perception of yourself and your capabilities.

IDENTIFYING LIMITING BELIEFS

2

I AM | I WILL | I CAN
I HAVE | I APPRECIATE

I AM MORE THAN MY
PAST EXPERIENCES AND
BELIEFS.

AFFIRMATION

I AM | I WILL | I CAN
I HAVE | I APPRECIATE

MEDITATION

Focus on your breathing, letting each breath guide you deeper into relaxation. Imagine each limiting belief as a weight that you've been carrying. With every breath, feel these weights becoming lighter, symbolizing your understanding and release of their impact. You can become supernatural through the transformation of your thoughts. Feel the power of your awareness to change your physical and emotional worlds.

WRITING

Choose a limiting belief and explore its effects on your life. How has it influenced your decisions, relationships, and self-image? Repeat the process for other beliefs if you choose, or return on a different day.

IDENTIFYING
LIMITING BELIEFS

3

I AM | I WILL | I CAN
I HAVE | I APPRECIATE

I POSSESS THE POWER
TO REWRITE MY STORY.

AFFIRMATION

I AM | I WILL | I CAN
I HAVE | I APPRECIATE

MEDITATION

Envision yourself in a space of infinite possibilities, surrounded by a luminous energy representing your highest potential. Within this space, affirm aloud that you are rewriting your story with beliefs that empower and uplift you. Visualize or feel each positive belief as a beam of light guiding you toward your desired reality. Feel the energy of your vortex of attraction, drawing to you the essence of what you seek.

WRITING

Contemplate the positive beliefs you wish to cultivate. How will adopting these beliefs transform your life? Drawing on the principle of "feeling as if it is already done" from Esther Hicks, document the changes in your daily life once these beliefs are fully integrated.

IDENTIFYING
LIMITING BELIEFS

4

I AM | I WILL | I CAN
I HAVE | I APPRECIATE

EVERY DAY, I AM
BETTER AND BETTER.

AFFIRMATION

I AM | I WILL | I CAN
I HAVE | I APPRECIATE

MEDITATION

Envision yourself in a space of infinite possibilities, surrounded by a luminous energy representing your highest potential. Within this space, affirm that you are rewriting your story with beliefs that empower and uplift you. Visualize each positive belief as a beam of light. Settle into a peaceful state of mind, focusing on your heart, where love and acceptance reside. Imagine each of your new affirmations as seeds planted in this fertile ground, nurtured by the coherent energy of your heart. As each seed grows, visualize yourself living out these affirmations, fully embodying their truth. Breathe in sync with your heart and your positive emotions. Your heart is in coherence, a powerful state for transformation and manifestation, guiding you toward your desired reality. Feel the energy of your vortex of attraction, drawing to you the essence of what you seek.

WRITING

Craft a personal affirmation that directly counters one of your limiting beliefs. Reflect on how this new affirmation feels more aligned with your true self and desires, tapping into the feeling of gratitude and appreciation for its realization.

IDENTIFYING
LIMITING BELIEFS

5

I AM | I WILL | I CAN
I HAVE | I APPRECIATE

I AM WORTHY OF MY
DREAMS AND CAPABLE
OF ACHIEVING THEM.

AFFIRMATION

I AM | I WILL | I CAN
I HAVE | I APPRECIATE

MEDITATION

Close your eyes and breathe deeply, centering yourself in the present moment. Envision transcending all limiting beliefs and living in alignment with your highest potential. Feel your best self fully immersed in the reality of your dreams. Imagine what you are doing, how you interact with the world, and the joy and fulfillment you feel. Feel the power of intention as your desires manifest through your best self. Feel it in every cell of your being, knowing it is within your reach.

WRITING

Describe who you are without your limiting beliefs. Focus on how it feels to live your dream life. Detail your activities, emotions, and the impact of this transformation on your relationships and self-perception. Embrace the feeling, knowing it's on its way to you now.

IDENTIFYING
LIMITING BELIEFS

6

I AM | I WILL | I CAN
I HAVE | I APPRECIATE

I RELEASE WHAT NO
LONGER SERVES ME
WITH EASE.

AFFIRMATION

I AM | I WILL | I CAN
I HAVE | I APPRECIATE

MEDITATION

Visualize, describe, or feel yourself standing at the edge of a serene body of water, holding stones representing your limiting beliefs. One by one, release them into the water, watching as they ripple away, stone by stone, symbolizing the release of these beliefs. With each stone thrown, feel lighter and more open to change. Release what no longer serves you to make room for new growth and opportunities.

WRITING

Write a goodbye letter to a limiting belief you are ready to let go of. Acknowledge its presence in your life and the lessons it taught you, then firmly declare your readiness to move beyond it. Recognize this release as essential in making space for your desires to manifest.

IDENTIFYING LIMITING BELIEFS

7

I AM | I WILL | I CAN
I HAVE | I APPRECIATE

I AM CONSTANTLY
GROWING AND
IMPROVING.

AFFIRMATION

I AM | I WILL | I CAN
I HAVE | I APPRECIATE

MEDITATION

Reflect on the past week's journey
with deep, grounding breaths.
Visualize the insights you've gained
and the shifts in your belief system as
light illuminating your path forward.
Set intentions for how you wish to
continue this journey of growth and
manifestation. Write them in the air,
in your mind, or say them aloud.
Imagine planting these intentions as
seeds in a garden, each one
representing a dream or goal you're
nurturing. Feel a sense of eagerness
and openness to how these intentions
will manifest in your life, embracing
the path of least resistance as you
align with your desires.

WRITING

Reflect on the insights and shifts you've experienced this week. How have your perceptions and beliefs changed? What intentions will you set for the coming weeks? How do you plan to nurture these seeds of desire? Consider how your intentions align with your highest self and the steps you'll take to embody this daily.

EXPAND

VISUALIZATION AND AFFIRMATION FOR EMPOWERMENT

VISUALIZATION AND AFFIRMATION FOR EMPOWERMENT

8

I AM | I WILL | I CAN
I HAVE | I APPRECIATE

MY VISION IS CLEAR,
AND MY MIND IS
FOCUSED ON
MANIFESTING MY
DREAMS.

AFFIRMATION

I AM | I WILL | I CAN
I HAVE | I APPRECIATE

MEDITATION

Find a quiet place to sit comfortably, close your eyes, and take deep, relaxing breaths. Begin to visualize a goal or desire you wish to manifest. Picture it, or narrate it in vivid detail, using all your senses. What does achieving this goal look like, feel like, sound like, taste like, and smell like? Dive deep into this meditation, feeling the emotions associated with your success as if it's happening right now. Create a new reality by vividly imagining or narrating aloud and feeling your desired future.

WRITING

Describe the goal or desire you visualize or narrate aloud in as much detail as possible. How does it feel to immerse yourself fully? What steps can you take today to align your actions with this vision? Reflect on your desire's emotional and sensory details, reinforcing the practice of "feeling as if it is already done."

VISUALIZATION
AND AFFIRMATION
FOR EMPOWERMENT

9

I AM | I WILL | I CAN
I HAVE | I APPRECIATE

EVERY DAY, MY ABILITY
TO CREATE MY SUCCESS
GROWS STRONGER.

AFFIRMATION

I AM | I WILL | I CAN
I HAVE | I APPRECIATE

MEDITATION

Continue your visualization practice, focusing on enhancing the clarity and detail of your vision. This time, introduce elements that symbolize the achievement of your goal, such as specific conversations, connections, events, or personal milestones. Feel these elements integrate into your energetic field. The power of attention, appreciation, and affirmation shapes your reality.

WRITING

Reflect on the details of your desire. How do these details contribute to your vision's vividness and emotional impact? Can you think of other sensorial elements that create a more vital emotion and memory? Write about these sensations and the feelings these enriched details evoke, and consider how they inspire action toward your goal.

VISUALIZATION AND AFFIRMATION FOR EMPOWERMENT

10

I AM | I WILL | I CAN
I HAVE | I APPRECIATE

OBSTACLES ARE
STEPPING STONES THAT
LEAD ME CLOSER TO THE
CLARITY MY DREAMS
REQUIRE TO MANIFEST.

AFFIRMATION

I AM | I WILL | I CAN
I HAVE | I APPRECIATE

MEDITATION

Visualize or narrate facing a challenge or obstacle on your path to achieving your goal. Imagine yourself navigating this challenge with wisdom, strength, and grace. Focus on the solutions and feel the support that comes your way, seeing yourself emerge victorious and strengthened by the experience. Feel your resilience and positive outcomes as obstacles transform into the catalysts for clarity in manifesting your desires.

WRITING

Think of an obstacle you recently overcame. Write about it. How did you navigate it, and what strengths did you discover or utilize? Reflect on how overcoming this challenge has brought you closer to your goal. How do you feel about it? Resilient? Empowered? Write five feelings to accompany this journal entry.

VISUALIZATION AND AFFIRMATION FOR EMPOWERMENT

11

I AM | I WILL | I CAN
I HAVE | I APPRECIATE

I CREATE AFFIRMATIONS
THAT REFLECT MY
WORTH AND GUIDE MY
JOURNEY TOWARD MY
HIGHEST SELF.

AFFIRMATION

I AM | I WILL | I CAN
I HAVE | I APPRECIATE

MEDITATION

Sit quietly and focus on your heart space, breathing deeply and evenly. Reflect on who you know yourself to be at a deep level. Bring into your awareness your core desires and the authenticity of who you are. Craft a personal affirmation for these desires and qualities. Use positive, present-tense language. Repeat this affirmation silently, feeling the truth resonate within you. You always have access to the energetic shift and transformative power of a deep knowing of the self combined with affirmations.

WRITING

Craft three powerful, personalized affirmations related to three different aspects of your life, such as health, relationships, or career. How do these affirmations make you feel? How can you integrate them into your daily routine to continually manifest your desires?

VISUALIZATION AND AFFIRMATION FOR EMPOWERMENT

12

I AM | I WILL | I CAN
I HAVE | I APPRECIATE

I LIVE THE TRUTH OF MY
AFFIRMATIONS,
ATTRACTING ABUNDANCE
AND JOY INTO MY LIFE.

AFFIRMATION

I AM | I WILL | I CAN
I HAVE | I APPRECIATE

MEDITATION

Begin your meditation by centering yourself with deep breaths. With each inhalation, envision yourself drawing in your creative energy, filling every cell of your body with power and positivity. Visualize or narrate yourself moving through your day, embodying your truth and connection to your deeper self in every action and decision. See the positive impact of living your desires, noticing how they attract experiences and opportunities that align with your deeper purpose. You become supernatural when you embody your desired state of being in the present moment.

WRITING

How does embodying and feeling your daily affirmations transform your experiences and interactions? How does living your affirmations change how you approach challenges, opportunities, and relationships? Identify specific ways to remind yourself to embody, feel, and sense your desires through daily affirmations.

VISUALIZATION AND AFFIRMATION FOR EMPOWERMENT

13

I AM | I WILL | I CAN
I HAVE | I APPRECIATE

I CONTINUE TO EVOLVE, GROW, AND ASCEND TOWARD MY HIGHEST ASPIRATIONS.

AFFIRMATION

I AM | I WILL | I CAN
I HAVE | I APPRECIATE

MEDITATION

Sit quietly, taking deep, relaxing breaths. Reflect on your current, favorite, or most used affirmations. How deeply do they resonate with your inner self? Go through the following phrases one at a time and see what inspiration follows.

I am_____. I can_____.
I will_____.
I have_____. I appreciate_____.

What does this tell you about your evolving desires and self-understanding? Thank yourself, and give love to yourself for taking this heart-centered step towards awareness and alignment with your inner being and desires for manifestation.

WRITING

Review the affirmations you've been working with. Are there any that no longer resonate or could be more powerful? Write new or revised affirmations that reflect your current growth and understanding. Align your writing with your deep self-image. Reflect on the process of evolving your affirmations and how they mirror your journey of self-discovery and manifestation.

VISUALIZATION AND AFFIRMATION FOR EMPOWERMENT

14

I AM | I WILL | I CAN
I HAVE | I APPRECIATE

I AM EMPOWERED,
CONFIDENT, AND FULLY
ALIGNED.

AFFIRMATION

I AM | I WILL | I CAN
I HAVE | I APPRECIATE

MEDITATION

In this meditation, focus on embodying a state of empowerment and confidence. Feel it. Visualize or narrate yourself achieving your goals with confidence and ease. See or narrate yourself moving through life empowered. Add as much detail as you can. Be in the moment and the feeling of everything you want, being here now. Feel the strength and certainty of aligning your thoughts, words, and actions with your deepest desires. Take the helm and manifest your desired reality now.

WRITING

Reflect on your experiences with feeling your desires. Reflect on your practices for visualization (or narration) and affirmation over the past week. How have these practices influenced your sense of empowerment and confidence? Write about specific instances where visualization/narration and affirmation have made a tangible difference in your approach to challenges or opportunities. Plan how you will continue to use these tools to nurture your empowerment and manifest your dreams.

EXEMPLIFY

ACTION AND
MANIFESTING
YOUR DREAMS

ACTION AND MANIFESTING YOUR DREAMS

15

I AM | I WILL | I CAN
I HAVE | I APPRECIATE

MY ACTIONS ARE
CONTINUALLY IN
PERFECT ALIGNMENT
WITH MY INTENTIONS.

AFFIRMATION

I AM | I WILL | I CAN
I HAVE | I APPRECIATE

MEDITATION

Sit comfortably and close your eyes. Take deep breaths to center yourself. Visualize or feel your intentions for your life as bright, glowing objects floating in space around you. One by one, reach out and touch each intention, feeling its energy. As you touch each one, see or feel a pathway lighting up from the intention to yourself, representing actions you can take to align with this intention. Imagine and feel that you are walking these paths with confidence and purpose, each step bringing you closer to your desired reality. Now, make your future dream a present fact through action.

WRITING

Reflect on the intentions you created
and the actions associated with them.
What are some specific, practical steps
you can take today to align your
actions with these intentions?

How do these actions make you feel in
terms of their alignment with your
overall desires?

ACTION AND MANIFESTING YOUR DREAMS

16

I AM | I WILL | I CAN
I HAVE | I APPRECIATE

MY THOUGHTS AND
ACTIONS ARE IN
HARMONY WITH MY
LIFE'S PURPOSE.

AFFIRMATION

I AM | I WILL | I CAN
I HAVE | I APPRECIATE

MEDITATION

Begin with a few deep breaths, finding a state of calm focus. Visualize or feel a beam of light from 400 feet above your crown, gently infusing you with focus and motivation. See or know that this light guides your path through your daily actions, keeping you aligned with your goals and preventing distractions.

Whenever you notice your focus wavering, bring in the warmth and love of this light. As it becomes brighter, it pulls you back on track with a gentle, encouraging force.

WRITING

Consider a beam of light filled with infinite possibilities and unconditional love as your focus and motivation. How can you cultivate and maintain this focus in your daily life? How will you support and care for yourself on this journey? Write about strategies to keep yourself motivated, especially when facing challenges, difficult emotions, or distractions.

ACTION AND MANIFESTING YOUR DREAMS

17

I AM | I WILL | I CAN
I HAVE | I APPRECIATE

I AM FLEXIBLE AND
OPEN, TRUSTING THAT
MY SOURCE GUIDES ME
TO MY HIGHEST GOOD.

AFFIRMATION

I AM | I WILL | I CAN
I HAVE | I APPRECIATE

MEDITATION

Find a comfortable, quiet place to sit.
Take deep breaths and allow yourself
to feel grounded and open. Imagine
you are a tree, any tree of your choice.
You are strong and rooted, yet flexible
and able to sway with the wind. You
can stay grounded in your intentions
while being flexible and open to the
opportunities and changes life brings.
Feel the excitement of the wind
bringing you messages as you accept
them with eagerness and gratitude.
Allow yourself to be guided to growth
and an inspired path forward. Stay
open, content, and flexible. Remember
that your source collaborates with you
to solve everything between you and
your deepest desires. Stay in the
energy of the greatest allowance and
open your heart to new possibilities
that align with your intentions.

WRITING

Reflect on the importance of flexibility and openness in your journey. How can being more fluid and mutable benefit you in pursuing your goals? Write about a time when being open to unexpected opportunities led to positive outcomes in your life.

ACTION AND MANIFESTING YOUR DREAMS

18

I AM | I WILL | I CAN
I HAVE | I APPRECIATE

I EFFORTLESSLY
ATTRACT EXPERIENCES
THAT MATCH THE
VIBRATION OF MY
DESIRES.

AFFIRMATION

I AM | I WILL | I CAN
I HAVE | I APPRECIATE

MEDITATION

Start by focusing on your breath, allowing yourself to relax and become receptive. Think about your greatest desire as already fulfilled. What does that feel like? Name and feel each emotion, allowing the energy to ripple through your body. Do you feel happiness? Contentment? Relief? Joy? Peace? Excitement? Confidence? Exuberance? Exhilaration? Accomplishment? Love? Appreciation? Throughout your day, seek out experiences, people, and thoughts that match feeling good. Continually revisit these vibrational sensations. This will reinforce the energetic match to your desire.

WRITING

Reflect on the feelings associated with your desires as already fulfilled. Throughout today, note any moments, interactions, or thoughts that matched this vibration. How did recognizing these moments make you feel?

ACTION AND MANIFESTING YOUR DREAMS

19

I AM | I WILL | I CAN
I HAVE | I APPRECIATE

I APPRECIATE EVERY
SUCCESS, NO MATTER
HOW SMALL, AS IT
PROPELS ME CLOSER TO
MY DREAMS.

AFFIRMATION

I AM | I WILL | I CAN
I HAVE | I APPRECIATE

MEDITATION

In a quiet space, breathe deeply and center yourself. Reflect on the small successes and positive moments you've experienced recently. Visualize or narrate each success as a light, buzzing vibration filled with love. Feel this love contributing to a brighter glow within you. As you feel the glow, feel the cumulative positive impact of these achievements on your journey. Feel appreciation and gratitude for these moments, understanding that each one is a step closer to your larger goals. Your dreams become a reality as you increase this appreciation and gratitude and take action.

WRITING

Write about the small successes you've recently experienced and any positive moments that stand out to you. Reflect on how these moments contribute to your larger goals and how they make you feel. Consider the vibrational match these successes provide to your overall desires, no matter how small. How will you be accountable for continuing to vibrate in alignment with your true self and deepest desires?

ACTION AND MANIFESTING YOUR DREAMS

20

I AM | I WILL | I CAN
I HAVE | I APPRECIATE

I EAGERLY ANTICIPATE,
OPEN, AND READY TO
RECEIVE THE ABUNDANCE
OF THE UNIVERSE.

AFFIRMATION

I AM | I WILL | I CAN
I HAVE | I APPRECIATE

MEDITATION

Focus on feeling eager anticipation for your desires. Unlike anxiety or impatience, this anticipation buzzes with inspired electricity, warming your heart. It is joyful and full of positive expectations. Declare yourself open and ready to receive, with arms wide open, facing the sky. Take a moment to desire, declare, claim, and deeply feel all you are manifesting.
Your wishes are moving gently towards you. Feel the excitement of their arrival. Expect miracles with openness.
Know they are yours.

WRITING

Contemplate the feeling of eager anticipation. Feel what you want as if it is already here. What emotions arise specific to what you are manifesting? How do feelings of openness and readiness to receive contrast with impatience or attachment?
Write about how you can cultivate a state of anticipation in your daily life, aligning with the path of least resistance...which is also the path of greatest allowance.

ACTION AND MANIFESTING YOUR DREAMS

21

I AM | I WILL | I CAN
I HAVE | I APPRECIATE

I AM PROFOUNDLY
GRATEFUL FOR THE
MANIFESTATION OF ALL
MY DESIRES CONSTANTLY
UNFOLDING IN MY LIFE.

AFFIRMATION

I AM | I WILL | I CAN
I HAVE | I APPRECIATE

MEDITATION

In a peaceful place, reflect on your journey over the past three to four weeks. Breathe deeply, filling yourself with a sense of accomplishment and gratitude. Give yourself appreciation. Feel love towards yourself. Be in this juicy gratitude for all you are until now and for all you are still creating. Recall the moments of insight, the shifts in perception, and the steps you've taken toward your desires. Feel a profound gratitude for your growth, the guidance you've received, and the manifestations on their way to you. Promise yourself to be in the vibration of deep appreciation today. Seek out people, places, and things that will vibrate with this love, and be proud of all you have done.

WRITING

Reflect on the last 21 days of your journey. What have you learned about yourself and the Law of Attraction? How have your perceptions and experiences shifted? How do you plan to continue applying these principles in your life? Make a list of actions that will support you moving forward. Write a list of people, places, and things you appreciate, as well as the feelings associated with gratitude in your journey so far. Finally, write your most prominent and specific desire you will move to next...and feel the energy and emotion that it is already here!

Thank you for embarking on this journey to trust yourself and the power of the Law of Attraction. As one person lifts energy to a higher vibration, the vibration is lifted for others, so thank you for being an integral part of that mission.

If this helped you, please share a quick review on Amazon. It's fast and easy, allowing others to benefit from the book. As a thank you for leaving a review, I have an incredible free bonus. To receive it, join our online community at http://www.facebook.com/groups/astrology4wellness

You will have immediate and exclusive access to free downloads, engaging Q&A sessions, and a tribe as dedicated as you are. Together, let's continue our journey toward bliss and abundance.

MAY ALL YOUR DESIRES BE MANIFESTED!

RESOURCES

Clear, J. (2018). *Atomic Habits: An easy & proven way to build good habits & break bad ones.* https://catalog.umj.ac.id/index.php?p=show_detail&id=62390

Dispenza, J. (2017). *Becoming Supernatural: How Common People are Doing the Uncommon.* Hay House, Inc.

Dyer, W. W. (2010). *The Power of Intention: Learning to Co-create Your World Your Way.* Hay House, Inc.

Hay, L. (1995). *You Can Heal Your Life.* Hay House, Inc.

Hicks, E., & Hicks, J. (2009). *Ask and It Is Given: Learning to Manifest Your Desires.* ReadHowYouWant.com.

Maltz, M. (2015). *Psycho-Cybernetics: Updated and Expanded.* Penguin.

Open AI. (n.d.). https://open.ai/

THANK YOU